BE A GIRL CHAMPION

BE A GIRL CHAMPION

Written and Illustrated by
Chloe Seraspe Reynaldo

Fort Worth, Texas

Library of Congress Control Number:2019943474

TCU Box 298300
Fort Worth, Texas 76129
817.257.7822
www.prs.tcu.edu
To order books: 1.800.826.8911

Design by Jan Ballard

discovering
global citizenship

CONTENTS

FOREWORD

I was seven years old when I learned that my Ol' Ma, my grandmother, could not read. This was in the early nineties before cell phones and high speed internet, and in order to communicate with my Ol' Ma in Liberia, my mother encouraged my sisters and me to write her letters from our home in Texas, which would then be read to her by family members. Most little girls like myself consider their grandmothers to be deities, fulcrums of love with healing powers even greater than those of our parents. In my fondest childhood memories, my Ol' Ma sits hunched over me and my sisters, telling us stories that wove in and out of the Vai language—stories with depth and posture, characters who traveled the world, who slayed monsters, who cast spells. She is the wisest woman I know. Although she never had formal education, she championed education among her children and grand-children. With the help of my grandfather, who was also a feminist in his own right, she enrolled her daughters into school in Monrovia, convinced that education was the key to independence and a fulfilled life. All five of her daughters finished college; a couple of her daughters even had Ivy League degrees and doctorates. And her granddaughter became a novelist. There was no way she could know then that the decision to champion edu-cation in her immediate family, something that wasn't done during her time among the Vai ethnic group from which she came, would change the trajectory of all of her descendants. It was that decision that changed my life.

Returning to Liberia as an adult, I quickly realized that my grandmother's story was an anomaly. Women's rights to education and agency are a constant fight in Liberia and in countries across the world, even in the United States. So, when I heard of the work of Chloe Seraspe Reynaldo and her fight for gender justice in the Philippines and across the world, I was ecstatic. The advocacy of young girls is exactly the kind of agent that will create critical and sustainable awareness about issues women face on a daily basis around the world. That we have to fight for education, that we have to fight for basic consideration in healthcare, that we have to fight for license to govern our own bodies, all basic human rights, is a genuine tragedy. The answer, the only answer, is to continue to blow our horns, to beat our drums, and to do anything we can to uplift each other in the international charge for women's rights and freedoms. Chosen as the youngest delegate and speaker for the UN Asia-Pacific Commemoration of International Women's Day 2016, Chloe has a number of notable accolades for her advocacy under her belt. She has been invited by UN Secretary General Ban Ki-moon to the World Humanitarian Summit in Istanbul, she's a member of Y-Peer, a global youth peer education initiative pioneered by the United Nations Population Fund, and she was an important resource and advocate for women and girls on adolescent sexual and reproductive health and rights, to name a few. But it is her commitment to dissecting the myriad issues plaguing young and under-served communities of women that is her greatest legacy.

Gender inequality is linked to illiteracy, poverty, the health and mortality of women and children, and many more consequences that shape not just the lives of those who are immediately affected by the injustice, but ultimately entire societies, and as a result, our world. This book is an essential, breathtaking resistance to these injustices. With stories all written and illustrated by Chloe herself, *Be a Girl Champion* is an admirable accomplishment for this young author and a significant tool for empowering women around the globe, especially young women who are just beginning to understand the intricacies of gender as it relates to their assumed place in the world. The indignities of gender injustice are vast, and it is through voices like Chloe's that the bright light ahead is crystallized. As my grandmother and many other women who have fought to empower their daughters can testify, the task of championing the equality of girls is both enormous and necessary. Chloe's voice and commitment are necessary. Her light is enormous, unbound. She has only just begun.

— Wayétu Moore

Acknowledgments

The author wishes to thank Edward McNertney
and TCU's Discovering Global Citizenship;
James English and Manochehr Dorraj, cochairs
of the Global Innovator's Initiative, for their
sponsorship; Jan Ballard, designer; and
TCU Press for their work on the book.

BE A GIRL CHAMPION

CARLA

She's sixteen. She's soft-spoken, she's
friendly, and she likes the color blue a lot.
When she smiles, it's a quiet sort of smile,
one you barely notice.

But maybe that's to be expected, considering
she didn't have much to smile about when
she was younger.

Carla's father died when she was much younger,
leaving her with practically no memory of him.
It had always been just her and her mother,
living and weathering life's hardships together.

All that had come to a halt
in June 2008.

That year, Typhoon Frank hit Aklan, the
province where Carla and her mother
lived. It was a Public Storm Signal 4-level
typhoon, and its fast approach had left
people little time to prepare. Carla and
her mother lived too far from their town's
designated evacuation center to make
it there before the typhoon hit, so they
were forced to tough it out in their tiny
home. Having raised Carla on her own
all those years, her mother considered
herself to be both Carla's mom and
dad, and she did everything she could
to protect her little girl, physically and
emotionally. She whispered words of
comfort into her ear, rubbed her shaking
body, and blotted out the worst of the
sounds. All the while, they huddled

together in the most secure corner of their hut, Carla's mother trying her utmost to keep the house from being torn apart.

The storm eventually passed, but the herculean effort involved in protecting her daughter had taken its toll on Carla's mother. She fell severely ill immediately afterward, never having been too healthy to begin with, and became too weak to provide for her child. So Carla took it upon herself to walk the two miles to the nearest evacuation center, traversing through debris and fallen trees, to try to get some aid for her ailing mother. The long walk was dangerous for a little eight-year-old girl even under the best of conditions, but she had pressed on, thinking of her mother.

Once she arrived at the center, she was greeted by chaos — frantic evacuees fighting for relief goods. Without an adult beside her, no one

paid any attention to the little girl who stood at the back, staring in disbelief at the scene and wondering despairingly how she would get any help. Meek and afraid, she had hung back from the group at first, then slowly worked her way to the front in the hope of getting someone to notice and help her.

It was several hours before she received help of any kind, and even then she had only been given a meager amount of supplies. Still, it was better than nothing, and she started back on the same long journey, hurrying back to her mother.

Returning to the tiny shack she and her mother called home, Carla eagerly called out to her mother. The light weight of the flimsy bag of supplies settled uncomfortably in her hands, growing heavier as she realized that no one was answering.

"Mama?" she called.

But nobody came.

Slowly, she pushed the door open.
There lay her mother, slumped over
on the floor. She was gone.

She was gone,
and Carla was alone.

That day, a young girl and her ailing mother
had been left to fend for themselves. The task
of getting supplies for the family had fallen on
an eight-year-old girl who had to travel over
dangerous terrain, alone and afraid. That day,
a little girl had tried to get help of any kind,
only to be ignored and pushed aside, helpless.
That day, a death and loss that could have been
prevented happened needlessly.

Carla's story is not unique. Many young girls in the Philippines have been forced to take care of themselves after losing parents or guardians to natural disasters. While Carla eventually found a home with her aunt, not all girls who fall victim to the same fate get a happy ending. All their stories and all their voices are equally important.

If you know a girl like Carla,

Listen to her.

Know her worth.

Be a Girl Champion.

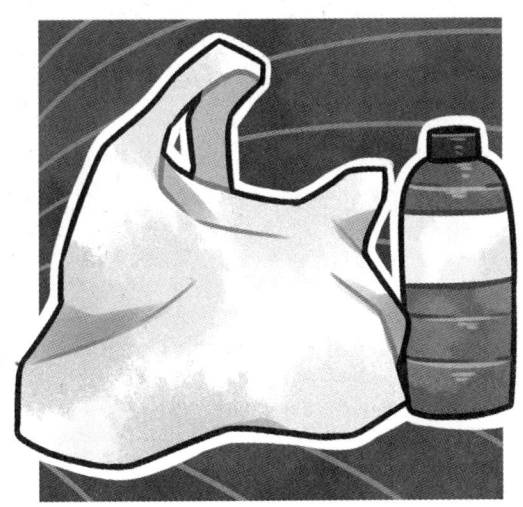

KOSUM

Kosum's interests are similar to those of other eight-year-old girls. She likes pretty things, playing with dolls, and most of all, she loves pink. However, unlike a lot of other girls her age, Kosum has to work to support her family. Every morning, she gets up at the crack of dawn to prepare breakfast for her family, lighting a fire by hand before getting shepherded to a day of hard work in the tea fields found in Northern Thailand. This is the only life she has known, and although it is hard, she finds satisfaction in the knowledge that she is helping to provide for her family.

However, things take a turn for the worse
a few days after her eighth birthday,
when her mother leaves their tiny home
and never returns.

Slowly but surely, things begin to change.

At first, Kosum tries to deny the reality of
what is happening. Surely her mother, who
stayed up until the wee hours of the morning
just to make sure her beloved children
would have proper clothing and food, would
never leave them. Kosum works hard in the
tea fields, harder than ever, but the loss of
her mother's income leaves a gap too big
to fill with her meager salary. It gets worse
when her father takes to drinking every
night, sometimes not even coming home.
Through all this, Kosum is left at home with
her younger siblings, wondering where their
next meal will come from, and slowly coming

to terms with the fact that their mother isn't coming back.

On the nights that her father manages to stumble home, Kosum retreats with her siblings into the small bedroom that they all share. One night, her father brings home a stranger. He calls Kosum out from the bedroom and introduces them — her father tells her that he's an old friend, one who has recently learned about their situation and is willing to help them.

The next day, there are new clothes waiting for Kosum as she arrives home from the tea fields. They're pretty, sparkling, and best of all, they're pink! She wonders who they could possibly be for, and her delight is immense when her father tells her that they're for her. When she puts them on, she feels like a princess — she prances around in the living room for her father and siblings, who all tell her she looks beautiful. Her

father even says that if she's good, she'll get more gifts. Her excitement only grows, and she wonders what sort of "help" her father's friend is going to give them.

That very night, Kosum's father approaches her and rubs a sweet-smelling oil around her neck and the back of her ears. It smells like jasmine, and she inhales the scent appreciatively, much better than the stale smell of alcohol that lingers pervasively around her father. His friend returns, and Kosum's father gently nudges her forward. Confused, Kosum only has time to see her father wave before the strange man ushers her out of her home.

He brings her to an old and dark building, where he leads her to a room full of other girls. Some are her age; some are older, some are younger. All of them look at her with resignation, and they turn away almost in

unison when the man comes back to fetch Kosum. She is brought to another, darker room, and shortly thereafter, a different man joins them. Her father's friend locks the door on his way out, leaving Kosum in the dark.

Kosum no longer works in the tea fields; instead, she waits each night for the man to fetch her from her home and bring her to the dark building. She goes about her menial household chores, anxiously fearing the sound of the man's footsteps as he approaches their home, which no longer feels safe or peaceful. She tells herself that she is doing this to provide for her family — that the health of her siblings and their well-being is worth what she has to do.

She keeps silent — a silence that is born of her childlike need for validation and attention from a parental figure, as well as her deep sense of duty to her family.

Kosum is just one of many girls in Thailand who have become victims of child trafficking and sexual exploitation. Many of them come from similar situations. Driven by poverty and desperation, families may sometimes sell their daughters off into brothels, and many girls, driven by both economic and social pressures, accept it as their duty.

Today, however, Kosum lives in Chiang Mai, in a shelter dedicated to girls who are at risk of or have been victims of trafficking, having been rescued from the brothel she had worked at. It's not easy to forget or move on from an experience like hers, but she tries hard to stay cheerful and optimistic. Kosum is grateful for the help she's received, and she hopes to be able to help other girls in situations like hers.

If you know a girl like Kosum,

Listen to her.
Know her worth.

Be a Girl Champion.

ANITA

"I don't understand any of this," Nadya grumbles, glaring at the pages of the biology textbook she's reading as they walk home from school. "If the cell is the smallest thing in the world, how did scientists see what they had inside? And why should we have to memorize all of them, anyway?"

"Actually, the cell is the smallest unit of life, not necessarily the smallest thing," Anita corrects her friend, smiling. "And they used microscopes to see inside of them and explain all the stuff that's going on inside the cells. We need to memorize them so that we understand how every living organism works and stays alive — and isn't it interesting anyway?"

"Maybe to you," Nadya retorts, but she smiles back. "You're so smart, Anita. You should be studying in some fancy school in Jakarta, not in a tiny village school."

"Maybe someday I will," Anita says dreamily. "And you're smart too, Nadya. You just don't like studying."

"Only you like studying, Anita."

The two friends reach Anita's home and part ways. Her mind still lost in their lesson, Anita barely notices her mother calling for her from the kitchen as she enters their home.

"Anita!" her mother calls. "Anita, come here!"

"Coming!" Anita calls back, snapping out of her reverie. Setting her bag down, she makes her way to the kitchen, where her mother and father are both waiting for her. "Father!" she exclaims, running to hug him. He rarely comes home this early, often staying late at his job. He chuckles as she hugs him tightly, but he's strangely quiet.

"What is it? You both look like you have something to tell me," Anita asks them, pulling away. "Did I do something wrong?"

"No, Anita, you did nothing wrong," her mother says, glancing at her husband. He takes his wife's hand and nods, signaling for her to continue. "We've called you to tell you that you won't be going to school anymore."

Anita freezes.

"One of your father's friends has offered an

engagement; he's made a proposal for your hand in marriage," her mother continues. "It would shame all of us, but especially you, if you were to reject his proposal. Your father told him that he would talk to you, but it's been decided that you will marry him."

Her father gently places his hand on Anita's shoulder. "He is a good man, Anita, and he will treat you well." He tries to meet her eyes, but her head is lowered, and she keeps silent.

Slowly, Anita shakes her head. "But . . . I don't want to get married," she says. "I don't want to quit school. I get good grades, I like being with my classmates, and my teachers all say that if I continue studying, I have a good chance of getting into a school in the city."

"But do you really want to study in the city?" her mother asks, trying to sound gentle.

"We can't afford to send you there even if you could get into a school. Besides, you were always going to get married; it's just a little earlier than any of us expected."

"But I don't even know him," Anita pleads, finally raising her head to look at her parents. She's trying hard not to cry, to defend her case as strongly as possible. "I don't want to marry someone I've never met. I want to go to school. I'm only fifteen!"

"Anita, it's been decided," her father says, looking softly at her even as his voice shuts down all protests. "You'll meet him soon, you can get acquainted, and you'll get married. You might even like him. I promise you, you'll get used to it. And we'll support you through it all."

"If you really supported me, you'd let me study,"

Anita counters bitterly, but she knows it's
no use; she needs to come to terms with this
new reality.

The next day, when Nadya comes to pick Anita
up, Anita's mother tells her that Anita is sick
and would not be going to school for some time.

—

Within a few days, Anita's new husband comes
to meet his girl bride and her family. He's a
man fifteen years her senior, a work friend of
her father's. When they are introduced, Anita
glances at him quickly and speaks as little as
possible to him. He doesn't seem to mind.

Within a week, he moves into their already
cramped home. Anita's parents try to make
him feel welcome even as Anita shrinks away
from him at every turn. In the end, however, her

husband's presence does little to change her daily life — except for the fact that she can no longer go to school.

At first, Anita tries to be strong. She keeps quiet as she watches her former classmates pass by her home on their way to school, hiding behind a curtain as she observes them discreetly. She helps her mother with chores, rubs her father's aching shoulders after long days at work, and tries not to speak to her husband if she can help it. He isn't even around all that much — most of the time, he leaves with Anita's father to work while she and her mother are left alone in the house. In her idle moments, Anita longs to return to school, but she knows that she would never be allowed. Local tradition in her little village dictates that once a girl receives a proposal, her family has to agree; otherwise, the girl would find it extremely difficult to find a husband in the future. In their own way,

her parents truly worry and care for her,
and since they thought this was what was
best for her, she had no choice but to follow.

But this doesn't stop her from wanting to learn.
She starts waking up in the middle of the night
and sneaking candles from the kitchen to read
her old textbooks in secret. It doesn't stop
her from contacting Nadya and swearing her
to secrecy, starting a covert correspondence
through which she receives notes from the
classes she could no longer attend. It doesn't
stop her from reading every book she can get
her hands on, every minute she could steal away,
reading and writing even as she lives unhappily
at home.

Just because I'm not in school anymore, she
reasons, doesn't mean I have to stop learning.

Three months into the farce of a marriage,

Anita begins to grow restless. Books and hastily
scribbled notes could only take her so far;
she longs for the feel of a pencil in her hand,
a teacher in front of her, and the four walls of
a classroom around her. Her parents are
becoming discontent as well; their son-in-law
often disappears at night to drink, frequently
taking money from his father-in-law to use.
He contributes little to the household, and is
slowly becoming a parasite.

One day, Anita could not stand it anymore.
She calls her mother to her bedroom as soon
as her father and husband leave for work.
"Mother," she began slowly. "I . . . I would like
to go back to school."

Her mother frowns. "Anita, it is impossible,"
she says gently. "I understand, I truly do, but
even if we let you go back, your school would not
accept you. Married girls cannot go to school."

"I know that," Anita says reluctantly. "But I want to go back. You know me, mother. You know that I have always loved to read, to study, to learn. I didn't want to marry this man, but I did because that is what you and Father wanted. I never wanted to give up my education. Look — " She takes a deep breath and leads her mother to her bed, under which she had hidden a small trunk. She pulls it out and opens it.

"I haven't stopped studying," she says quietly, pulling out the textbooks she had been reading and rereading to show to her mother. One by one, she lays out the notebooks Nadya had given her. "Even if I couldn't leave the house, I studied as if I was in school." She grasps her mother's hands. "Mother, please."

"Oh, Anita," murmurs her mother, looking over her young daughter's work. She looks up, her eyes shining. "I'll see what I can do."

That night, Anita's mother pulls her father aside as soon as he comes home from work. Their son-in-law is nowhere to be found. Anita stands outside the door, straining to hear their conversation. When they come out, Anita's father looks at her sternly; then his eyes soften and he bends down to embrace his daughter. "We love you very much, Anita," he whispers. "We will do all that we can."

Anita's heart soars.

—

In the days that follow, Anita's parents spend their time at her old school, pleading their daughter's case. The school board is initially adamant on the matter, refusing to allow Anita back in. But when the girl herself finally comes to defend herself, showing how she had kept up with her studies, they relent. Anita can finally return to school.

—

"I hate science," Nadya grumbles, glaring at the pages of the biology book she's reading as they walk home from school. "How am I supposed to remember which parts plant cells have and animal cells don't?"

"Actually, it's pretty simple," Anita assures her, smiling. "You just have to remember which parts they both have, and memorizing their different parts should be easy."

"Maybe to you," Nadya retorts, but she smiles back. "Welcome back, Anita."

—

Today, Anita is studying in Jakarta, studying hard to keep her scholarship and to get a job, just as she had dreamed when she was younger. Her husband has moved out of her family's home and does not communicate with them. Enrolling at the university had presented her with challenges and obstacles, just as initially returning to school had, but as before, she didn't have to face them alone. She wouldn't be alone again.

If you know a girl like Anita,

Listen to her.
Know her worth.

Be a Girl Champion.

CHANMALI

"Why can't I go to the plantations?"

At least once a week, Chanmali would ask the same question, watching her friends through the window as they passed her home. She doesn't even really know what the word "plantation" means; all she knows is that everybody else her age would go to the plantations after school, standing off to the side as the workers and some foreign men tilled the field and brought in banana suckers to plant in the soil. It was interesting, but her mother would never allow her to go with her friends.

"I don't trust those strange men," her mother would reply every time, dismissing Chanmali's pleas and instructing her to finish her chores instead. "And besides, why would you even want to go and watch them work when you could just stay here at home?"

It's so unfair, Chanmali thinks, even as she obediently goes about her daily chores. All her other friends get to go and watch the workers in the fields; her friend Vatsana's family had even gone together once. There were big changes taking place in their tiny Lao village, and she could only get second-hand accounts of everything that was happening.

"It's so cool," Vatsana would tell her. "They have all these machines and everything. We're not allowed to go near the field, but one time they let us explore and see all the banana plants growing. They even gave us some coins! You should come, too."

"No," would be the firm reply of her mother. "Your father already works there all day; who would help me around the house if you wasted your time just watching in the fields?"

Chanmali could only sulk.

As the weeks pass, more and more foreign men start appearing in their village; the previously overgrown footpaths become downtrodden as workers flow in and out of the town. Banana plants sprout and flourish in the fields, transforming the bleak area into a verdant green. Although her mother remains adamant about not allowing her to go to the plantations, other changes begin to appear in Chanmali's life. She notices more food on their table; they eat better and more often. Her baby brother gets sick less often. She starts getting new clothes.

Most of all, there are bananas. Everywhere.

Bananas piled high on the table, whole bunches being driven past in large trucks; the yellow fruit becomes an integral part of daily life in their village. Chanmali eats bananas at breakfast, lunch, and dinner; she mashes bananas to feed to her baby brother, who eats it all enthusiastically. With every banana that she eats, her curiosity grows; what is it like in the banana plantations?

One day, Chanmali wakes up to the sound of knocking on their door. Judging from the pale color of the sky, it's still early; her mother must still be asleep. She walks quietly to the door and finds Vatsana waiting outside for her, carrying a dish.

"Hi," she greets Chanmali. "My mother made too much khao niao last night and remembered that your father likes it. She told me to bring some for him today before he leaves for the fields."

"How nice of her!" Chanmali says. "But I don't think Father is here right now, I think he already..." She pauses. Had her father come home last night? Had he come home the night before that, or before?

When is the last time she had seen
her father, anyway?

Vatsana watches her grow silent, concerned
and slightly confused. "Well, take it anyway.
You can bring back the dish whenever."
She pushes the slightly warm dish into
Chanmali's hands and leaves.

Slightly dazed, Chanmali retreats to their little
kitchen to put the dish away. True, she had been
seeing her father less and less recently. But she
had always thought that he simply got home late
at night and then left before they woke up. Her
mother hasn't said anything, so she hasn't asked.

"Chanmali?" her mother calls out, as she steps
out of the room she shares with her husband.
"Who was at the door?"

"Vatsana. She brought over some khao niao,"
Chanmali answers. "Mother, where is Father?'

The suddenness of the question catches her
mother off guard, who stiffens before sagging
slightly. "Did Vatsana say something about your
father?" she asks Chanmali, suddenly seeming
older and more tired.

Chanmali shakes her head. "No. Just that
the food was for Father."

Her mother comes over to her and takes her
hand. "Chanmali, your father is . . . he's still
at the field. But he's sick. He's been working in
the fields for weeks, and something is making
him ill. The strange men . . . they cover the land
in chemicals and fertilizers and it's not good
for his health."

"Is Father alright?" Chanmali asks automatically, thinking of her hardworking father. "Does he get enough rest? Can he come home?'"

"I think your father is alright for now," her mother answers carefully. "He sends messages through the neighbors. But a lot of the men are getting sick. The chemicals get into their food, their water . . . they're complaining to the strange men but they don't listen." She embraces Chanmali, pulling her close. "Chanmali, your father will be fine, but whatever you do, don't go to the plantations, okay?"

Chanmali is silent; then she hugs her mother back, wondering what will happen to them from here on out.

—

In 2014, Chinese investors arrived in Bokeo, a tranquil village in northern Laos. They offered villagers up to $720 per hectare to rent their land. They wanted to grow bananas there, for export. In impoverished Bokeo, the offer was highly attractive. The Chinese brought them a livelihood and higher wages, but they also drenched the plantations with pesticides

and other harmful chemicals. Workers like Chanmali's father who brave the manual labor at the plantations work themselves into illness and are laid off, with fewer job prospects than before.

Today, Chanmali is studying in Vientiane, the capital of Laos. Her father has saved up enough during his employment to put her through a few years of school, and Chanmali plans to earn her way through the rest. Her father now stays at home with his wife and their son, earning his living through carpentry. Chanmali says she'd like to study law, and to become a lawyer.

"Back then, nobody could fight for us; none of us would stand up for ourselves because we didn't know any better," she says. "That's why I want to become a lawyer, so I can help my village and hopefully help other people know their rights so that the same thing doesn't happen again."

If you know a girl like Chanmali,

Listen to her.
Know her worth.

Be a Girl Champion.

KANNITHA

Kannitha taps her perfectly manicured nails against the arm of the bench she's sitting on. Her long hair falls in a silky black curtain down her back. She pulls out her compact mirror to check her makeup one last time—yes, it's still perfect. She puckers her pink lips slightly and puts the mirror away.

Ten minutes, she thinks to herself.
Ten minutes, and then four hours,
and you'll be home.

Looking around her, it's plain to see that
Kannitha is easily the most beautiful girl
around. She can get away with wearing a simple
blouse and skinny jeans, while other girls have
to resort to wearing tight dresses and shorts.
Beside her, another girl—Davi, she remembers—
fussily primps her hair, then gives Kannitha
a nasty look when she catches her staring.
Kannitha hastily looks away.

Most of the other girls who work around here
either don't like her, or don't care about her one
way or another. Davi is one of the few
who openly dislike her, which makes sense—
Davi is one of the less popular beer girls
who frequent this particular bar.

Patrons are already milling about, waiting for
the bar to open. It's located in a nicer part of
Siem Reap, and thus has more regulated hours
and a better atmosphere than some other

places. A couple of men side-eye Kannitha—she smiles at them, flashing her pretty teeth. They chuckle good-naturedly and go back to their conversations. Before the bar actually opens, she usually screens the crowd for potential customers, making sure to smile at every person she makes eye contact with. Her livelihood depends on these people, these tourists; she could not let a single one slip away.

The bar opens shortly afterwards, letting in the night's customers. Kannitha stands up and walks in after the people, smiling brightly as a tall stranger wraps his arm around her waist and says, "Well, hello there, gorgeous."

—

"You should try this beer," Kannitha says, speaking over the loud dancing music. "It's a new taste, a good one."

English had never felt natural on her tongue, but this group of American tourists don't seem to mind. "Really?" one says. He has the same brown curls as the tall stranger who'd followed her in just an hour ago. He'd bought a hefty batch from her, and she's hoping this one would do the same. "How good?" he asks, smiling.

"Very good!" Kannitha says, laughing. Her friends have always told her she has a pretty laugh, a pretty smile. "Try, try it!"

"What do you say, boys?" the tourist asks, turning to his friends. "Should we buy some?"

"Of course they will say yes," Kannitha says, playfully punching him in the arm, the way she'd seen other girls do. "Don't you want to taste the good beer?" she asks them, batting her eyelashes.

"We'll buy a round if you'll drink with us!"
one tourist calls out, followed immediately by
laughter and hooting from the group. Kannitha
laughs with them.

Her smile falters when she notices another
beer girl pass by them, accompanied by a tall
American man. His arm is wrapped loosely
around her waist, and he leads her out of the
crowded bar and into the night. Kannitha
manages to tear her eyes away from them,
turning her attention back to the group of men
still trying to cajole her into drinking with them.

"You have to pay for my drink," she says,
wagging her finger playfully and grinning
when they groan. "It's the rule!"

The group laughs as they scoot over on the
circular bench they've all been sharing to make
room for her. She ends up sitting next to the

curly-haired brunette, who immediately places an arm around her shoulders. Kannitha does her best not to immediately shrug it off. "Get us a round, a round or two," he says, smiling.

Kannitha beams. "Okay, sure!"

—

Good nights mean that she manages to sell a lot of beer and maybe sneak away with a couple of tips. Good nights mean that at the end of the night, she emerges relatively untouched, maybe a little rustled and mussed but otherwise no worse than she had been at the beginning of the night. Good nights mean that she can walk home to her tiny apartment, and the only thing she has to do is wash her face before she falls asleep.

Tonight is a good night. Kannitha exhales

a deep sigh of relief as she watches the last
patron stumble out of the bar. She fixes
her blouse and hair before leaving the
establishment as well, the events of this
evening playing back in her mind.

That last guy had grabbed her wrist a little
too hard as he pulled her over to a table.
At least he had let go of her immediately.
And she's sure that someone had pulled on
her blouse as she had made her rounds around
the club. But it hadn't led to anything, so she'd
just walked a little faster, and everything had
been fine.

Everything is fine.

Her mind flashes briefly to the girl in the bar,
the one who'd left with that man.

Kannitha exhales again.

She hopes tomorrow night will be
another good one.

—

Kannitha is aware that there are girls who
do more than just sell beer. She has seen
customers lead girls outside, with their arms
around them. She hadn't really understood
what happened to the girls, until one night.

It had happened at the old bar she used to go
to — she'd taken more than a couple of drinks
in her quest to get more people to drink. A
male customer, handsome and friendly, had
agreed to buy more beer from her if she'd
agree to his request. Inebriated and eager to
please, she had followed, hardly noticing how
drunk the man himself was.

He hadn't even taken her outside. He'd led her to the bathroom—the men's bathroom—and pushed her into a stall. What happened next was painful and unpleasant, and when he'd finished, he'd drunkenly thrown a couple of dollar bills to her and left before she could even put her clothes back on. As she struggled to put herself together, she heard him slur out "Thanks," and stumble out of the bathroom.

She didn't leave the stall for a long time.

When she finally did, Kannitha wiped the tear tracks on her face, gathered her things, and left the bar. She would never return.

—

As she watched the girl leave with that man, a part of her regretted not interfering.

A bigger part of her had simply hoped that it would be a good night.

—

Today, Kannitha remains in Siem Reap, still hopping from bar to bar every night. She still works at her favorite bar, but with new guidelines set in place for the protection of beer girls such as herself, she feels safe enough to try branching out once more. Whenever she sees new girls in the clubs, shy and uncertain in the face of loud strangers, she sees her old self in them, and hopes that no one goes through what she has.

If you know a girl like Kannitha,

Listen to her.
Know her worth.

Be a Girl Champion.

TAM

Before mama or papa,
Tam's first word is "Hello."

She's a hopelessly affectionate baby, eager to
reach out to any and every visitor who enters
their small home in the northwestern village
of Sa Pa, Vietnam. Aunts and uncles delight in
her chubby cheeks and grabby hands, basking
in her affection.

Even as she grows up, Tam never loses her
love of befriending new people. Every stranger
is a potential friend. Her parents find it both

charming yet incredibly frustrating, worried that her blind trust in people could one day get her in trouble. More than once, her mother had had to pull her away from conversations with strange men in the markets, just one moment before she followed them to a more secluded place in the village or entered their homes.

"Tam, you mustn't follow strangers," her mother would say firmly. She despairs over Tam, who seems incapable of following this one simple rule. Her two sisters, one younger and one older, are both much more reserved and cautious. Tam, at nine, simply couldn't get it into her head that not everyone could be trusted.

"But what if they want to show me something?" she would ask. "What if they want to give me candy, or ice cream, or a dress? What if they have a cute doll that they would let me play with?"

"You have dolls here, and food," her mother
would say, knowing full well that Tam would
never take a simple "no" for an answer.
"Sometimes people pretend to be nice, Tam,
but not everyone in the world is kind. Some
of them may want to take you away from us,
from your family."

Still, Tam does not understand. "Why would
they take me away? That's not very nice."

"Not very nice" is a huge understatement.
Still, Tam's mother had no idea what to
do with her clueless daughter. Instead,
she implores her other daughters to keep
an eye on their sister.

Despite this, Tam persists. No longer allowed
to talk to strange men, she befriends their
children. Her pretty face and enthusiastic smile
endear her to girls and boys alike, increasing

her number of playmates exponentially. It seems like there isn't a single child in the village that Tam hasn't befriended, and her mother, although still worried, is nevertheless glad that her daughter has seemed to lose interest in talking to older strangers.

Things are quiet for a while, that is, until Tam turns fifteen and receives a smartphone.

Even the rural little community that Tam and her family live in isn't exempt from the technological revolution. Suddenly, their world expands beyond the reach of their small villages, far into Vietnam, and even into the rest of the world.

Like many others her age, Tam discovers Facebook and is instantly hooked. A platform that enables her to meet hundreds, no, thousands of other people her age?

It's everything she has ever dreamed of.
Her parents, who have no idea how to interact
with the social media platform, are once again
worried that this would become a point of
concern. However, their other daughters assure
them that Facebook is relatively safe. It isn't
as if they're meeting in real life, they reason,
and anytime someone would bother them,
they could easily leave the conversation or
block them from contacting them again.

Tam is overjoyed. Now, she has friends
from all over Vietnam, not just in her little
town. She has all the friends and admirers
a girl's heart could desire, including many
boys her age drawn to her pretty face.

One of them, however, is special.

His name is Minh, a city boy from Hanoi, and
his profile shows a handsome boy around

Tam's age with bright, friendly eyes and an attractive dimple on the right side of his face. His messages to her are always just slightly flirtatious, generous with compliments and affection. Tam finds herself growing attached to him, looking forward to his messages and checking her phone several times a day to see if he has sent her anything. Her sisters tease her good-naturedly about her crush, and although her mother frowns a little when she forgets her chores while chatting with Minh, she says nothing about it.

Minh is—charming, there's no other word for it. Although he lives far from her home in Sa Pa, she daydreams constantly, hoping that one day they could meet in person.

Imagine her shock and joy when he messages her on Facebook one day, saying that his family would be taking a trip near Sa Pa! She could

hardly believe it. When he asks her if she could show him around the town for a bit, maybe walk around with him, she wastes no time in typing out her agreement.

Her sisters laugh at her dreamy expression, but her parents worry. Tam is quick to reassure them that she would stay in the town and stay where people can see them. She's about to meet Minh, and she would do anything to ensure her parents allow her to see him. They reluctantly give her permission, hoping that if they allow this one time, it would dissuade her from meeting any of her other online friends.

Finally, the day comes when Minh is to visit her village. Tam can barely contain her excitement. She spends the morning dressing up, wanting to make sure she's as pretty as possible. When the time comes for her to meet him in the village central, she's literally bouncing on her feet with excitement.

"You sure are eager," her older sister Hue commented, noting the pink flush in Tam's cheeks. Tam only nodded, beaming. She's so excited!

Ten minutes before they're supposed to meet, Tam's already at their meeting place. People stop by to chat with her, finding her uncharacteristically distracted—even as they talk to her, her eyes wander.

When Minh finally shows up, Tam is instantly smitten. He's just as handsome and charming in real life as he is online, only this time they're talking to each other for real. He dresses well, as one would expect of a city boy, and he's taller than she had expected somehow, broader—but Tam just finds that even more attractive. As they

walk around the village, Tam finds that she can't keep her eyes off him, hanging onto his every word and gesture.

They walk around the village, and as small as it is, they quickly run out of attractions to see. "Want to go for a ride?" Minh eventually suggests. He had brought his motorbike, he explains, which he used to come to the village from the hotel he and his family are staying at.

Tam hesitates. This sounds like something her mother would be against. Just as she's about to say no, Minh flashes his charming, dimpled smile. "Come on," he says. "It's just a short ride."

How could she say no?

—

Witnesses later reported that Tam had last been seen getting onto a motorbike with a tall man none of the other villagers had seen before that day. Just before she had gotten onto the bike, Tam had called her older sister, saying that she would be home soon.

—

Tam is but one of many unknowing Vietnamese girls who have been kidnapped or lured away by human traffickers pretending to be friendly figures. Most of them are taken to be sold up north in China as either laborers or wives for Chinese men. Young, pretty girls like Tam are considered to be "prized commodities" due to the scarcity of marriageable young women in China.

However, Tam is one of the lucky ones. Her abductor, a twenty-five-year-old man who had been nowhere the age he was pretending to be, happened to take a break just as they were approaching the Chinese border. Taking advantage of his laxness, Tam had quickly run off, paying no heed to his threats as he chased after her. Eventually, she had come across a Chinese couple who recognized the situation and shielded her from her captor, who immediately ran off. They then accompanied her to a police station, helped her contact her family, and ensured she would be taken home.

Today, Tam is living peacefully with her family. She is still one of the prettiest and most cheerful girls in the village, and no one outside of her family knows the full story of her temporary disappearance. She still spends time with her friends, still talks to every acquaintance she crosses paths with. But she is careful and wary now, because she knows how lucky she was to be able to return. For every girl who manages to get home, there will dozens of others who are lost, others whose cases will go unheard.

If you know a girl like Tam,

Listen to her.
Know her worth.

Be a Girl Champion.

VALERIE

"How are your grades?" her mother asks

bluntly, picking apart the chicken on her plate.

Valerie looks up, surprised by the question.

"The same as usual," she replies, a bit

startled by the suddenness of the query.

"I still make perfect scores. We just had

a math exam yesterday—I'm sure I aced it."

Her mother nods, absently stabbing a piece

of chicken with her fork. "You're fine without

a tutor?"

"Yes, Mom." Valerie prides herself on her solid studying habits. She hasn't needed a tutor since she finished elementary—unlike most of her classmates, who often go to study centers or have their own tutors. Maybe Mom had talked to one of her classmate's mothers about this—it could be why she's asking. "I'm ranked first in our class."

Her mother breaks into a small smile at that, eyes glowing softly with pride. "Great job, Val," she says. "Your father and I are very proud of you."

Valerie returns the smile, only to be interrupted as her little brother starts to get restless in his high chair. "It's okay," she immediately says, rising from her seat before her mother can. "I've got him."

She lifts Alex out of his high chair and starts

to coo at her two-year-old brother. "Shh, shh. Do you want some chicken? Do you want some carrots?" she asks, speaking in a high-pitched voice. It doesn't really matter what she says to the baby, so long as he hears a soothing and familiar sound. Within seconds, he's reduced to a happy, giggly little toddler, all previous agitation gone. Valerie grins when he tries to grab her hair and puts him back in the high chair beside their mother. Their father's place at the table is empty—he's probably working late again.

"You've gotten good with him" her mother observes as she returns to her seat. Valerie only smiles.

—

Valerie remembers a time when she had been very young, still small enough that when she

would hug her mother, she'd have to wrap her
arms around a pair of legs. She had hugged
her mother whenever she had the chance back
then, because she rarely had the chance—during
daytime when she was awake, her mother would
be at the office, and she would always be asleep
by the time her mother got home. On weekends
or on holidays, Valerie would spend the whole
day attached to her mother, refusing to even let
her out of her sight.

Her father had played a larger role in her
childhood than her mother had. He'd also had
a job, but it had been less time-consuming and
demanding than her mother's. He had been
the one to drive her to and from daycare and
elementary, the one who had accompanied her
to various after-school activities and to her
piano recitals.

Now, it's as if her parents have switched

places—her mother has begun spending more time at home while her father spends more time at work.

Valerie looks up from the block of text that she's been reading over and over for the past minute or so. It isn't like her to be unfocused while studying, especially while studying English, one of her favorite subjects. She stands up from her desk and stretches, deciding to take a break.

She wanders out of her room to the kitchen, where her mother is seated at one of the counters. She doesn't notice Valerie, absorbed in the reports she's poring over. She only looks up when Valerie moves behind her to get something from the fridge. "What is it?" she asks her daughter.

"I'm hungry," Valerie responds, shrugging. She fills a glass with cold water and takes an apple out of the fridge. "I'm taking a break from studying."

"Are you having a hard time?" her mother asks, frowning. "Do you want me to make you something?"

"No, I'm fine. My eyes are just tired."
She walks over to her mother, looking at the papers her mother is currently going over and setting down her snack. "What is all this?"

Her mother rolls her eyes. "Mr. Li couldn't be bothered to finish his financial reports, so of course it falls onto me to clean up after him," she says, exasperated. "I swear, if I have to handle another one of his mistakes . . . "

Valerie feels her brow furrowing. "Mr. Li? Isn't he younger than you?" She remembers seeing him when she had been younger—

he's five or so years younger than her mother and had started working under her when Valerie had still been in elementary. He had been pleasant and friendly, and Valerie doesn't remember hearing him described as lazy.

"Yes, but he's higher-ranked," her mother sighs, missing the slight widening of Valerie's eyes. "So he can do whatever he wants and push anything on us. He's not bad, considering the past managers, but he sure can get lazy when he feels like it."

"He's your manager?!" Valerie repeats, confused. Unless her understanding of office life is completely wrong, she's sure the only way a younger, more junior employee could end up above her mother was if they were absolutely incredible at their job, or if her mother wasn't the best at her job. The way her mother describes Mr. Li makes the first option unlikely, and as for the possibility that her mother could be anything but excellent—it wasn't possible.

"He was promoted a couple of years ago," her mother affirms, more focused on the stack of papers than on the conversation. "And he's gotten a bit overconfident. He's managing now, but we're getting a big client soon, and when— if—it all falls apart, he's definitely going to shove the work onto the team again."

Valerie shakes her head, still unable to grasp a vital part of the situation. "But I don't get it. Why was he promoted instead of you? Shouldn't you be his boss?"

This question finally seems to get her mother's attention. She sits up and puts the papers down, looking at Valerie through thick glasses. "He led a couple of projects excellently well a few years back," she says, eventually turning back to the reports. "He may be less productive now, but the higher-ups liked to directly reward good performance, so he got promoted."

That still doesn't make sense—in fact, it raises more questions. If the higher-ups like to reward good performance, then why hasn't her mother gotten promoted? She's a hard worker, good at what she does, and an effective leader. That's the entire reason she had been gone so often. In fact, her father had once joked that her mother had been so good at her job that her bosses didn't want to let her go home.

"But she's my mama, not theirs!" Valerie had protested back then. Why did those people have to keep her mama? They should get their own.

Her father had only laughed, easing their car into the parking lot. It would be her very first recital, and her mother couldn't be there to watch her play. "Your mama's very, very good at her job. One day, she'll be the boss—and then she can come to all of your recitals."

"I just wish Mama could spend more time with us," Valerie grouched, but she got out of the car without further complaint.

Valerie would eventually get her wish. As soon as her mother had gotten pregnant with Alex, she'd started spending more time at home. Valerie had been ecstatic — thrilled with the prospect of spending more time with her mother, she had hovered around her, spewing endless questions about her coming sibling. Is it a boy or a girl? Ooh! What if it's twins? Is it kicking yet?

Her mother had laughed at her questions, and Valerie sighs even now just thinking about those times. To be honest, it's one of the reasons she's so attached to her little brother—his birth had marked a turning point in all their lives. Valerie had become an older sister, her father had been promoted shortly thereafter to a senior position, and her mother—her mother simply started staying home and talking less and less about work. In fact, today is the first time Valerie's heard anything important about her mother's job.

However, the conversation is clearly over. Her mother has returned to poring over the reports, a trivial task that she could easily have passed onto someone else, should have passed onto someone else. Sighing, Valerie eats her snack and drinks her water. Without another word, she returns to her room and picks up where she had left off.

As she reads the passage repeatedly, none of it registering in her brain, a tiny thought forms inside her head. Could this be why her mother is so focused on Valerie's success? Why she always monitors her study habits, her scores, her performance? Why she always has this image of Valerie being perfect?

So that Valerie could be what her mother could have been, but is not?

Briefly, Valerie wonders what her mother could be now, if Alex hadn't been born. If Valerie hadn't been born.

She could easily be as high-ranked as her father. Maybe even higher. Maybe her mother could have been the president of her own company if she hadn't had to give it up for them. She could have been insanely successful, responsible only for her own destiny.

Valerie shakes her head. But at what cost?

So instead, she clears her mind and focuses on studying. She focuses on being the best that she can possibly be. She focuses on what the future holds, instead of musing on what could have been.

She quietly promises herself that she would be what her mother could not.

—

Today, Valerie is studying hard for Singaporean college entrance exams, aiming to earn a high enough score to get into the National University of Singapore Business School. Although the pressure is high, she's confident that she'll be able to achieve her goals, especially since she's doing it with her family in mind.

"I want to repay everything that my parents have given to me—my comfortable lifestyle, my education, and their unending support," she says. "I owe everything that I achieve to them, and this will be no different. Nothing will stop me from attaining my dreams. Absolutely nothing."

If you know a girl like Valerie,

Listen to her.
Know her worth.

Be a Girl Champion.

Photo by Kylie Fales Crane

ABOUT THE AUTHOR

Chloe Seraspe Reynaldo

Chloe started writing and drawing at four years old, about princesses, but with a modern twist. She gave her first public speech also at four years old as top graduate of her kindergarten class. From there she went on to higher highs, consistently reaping academic honors and awards throughout elementary and high school. She spoke at international events on the issues she holds dear: gender equality and adolescent sexual and reproductive health. In 2016, she received the Global Innovator Prize from Texas Christian University (TCU). Now a student on her way to becoming a surgeon, Chloe shares her advocacy, passion, and heart through this little book.

TCU Global Innovators Initiative Cochairs, Manochehr Dorraj (TCU Political Science) and James English (TCU International Services), present the Global Innovator Prize to Chloe Seraspe Reynaldo on campus in Texas. *Photo by Claire Hargis.*

Discovering Global Citizenship

The Global Innovators Initiative at TCU partners ground-breaking individuals from throughout the world with faculty, staff, and students on long-term projects that address critical global issues.

The initiative seeks to support the work of individuals who are actively engaged on the front lines of major global challenges. Chloe partnered with Jan Ballard (TCU Department of Design) on this collection of stories about young women in Southeast Asia, which aims to provide teens worldwide with positive stories of youth empowerment and gender equality.